The Desert Run

John Bonallack

Learning Media

Contents

1. *A Fantastic Adventure*

"The toughest footrace on earth!"

Well, they say that about a lot of races. But this race, the Marathon des Sables,* looked like a big challenge.

Marathon des Sables

- 143 miles long
- 7 days in the Sahara Desert
- temperature up to 120°F during the day, down to freezing at night
- runners carry all their own food and gear for the week

It sounded like a fantastic adventure for Dan and me!

We started training nine months before the race. We ran with rucksacks, and we did a lot of hill work – up to 60 miles a week!

* That's French for "Marathon of the Sands."

Then the race rules and equipment lists arrived in the mail.

We needed:

- Lightweight runner's rucksack
- Sunglasses
- Sunhat with neck flap
- Sunblock
- Running shoes, socks, shorts, shirt
- Water bottles
- Lightweight sleeping bag
- Flashlight (for running at night)
- Compass, whistle, reflector mirror
- Camping stove, fuel tablets, matches
- Plate, spoon, Swiss army knife
- Anti-venom pump (for scorpion or snake bites)
- Dried food and high-energy drink powder
- First-aid kit and salt tablets
- Wash kit, toilet paper

We spread all the gear out on the floor. Then we tried to stuff it into our rucksacks. It wouldn't fit, and it was far too heavy. We cut back and cut back. Only one shirt, one pair of shorts, and one pair of socks for the week. No underpants. No wash kit .... Even then, we ended up with about twenty-five pounds each.

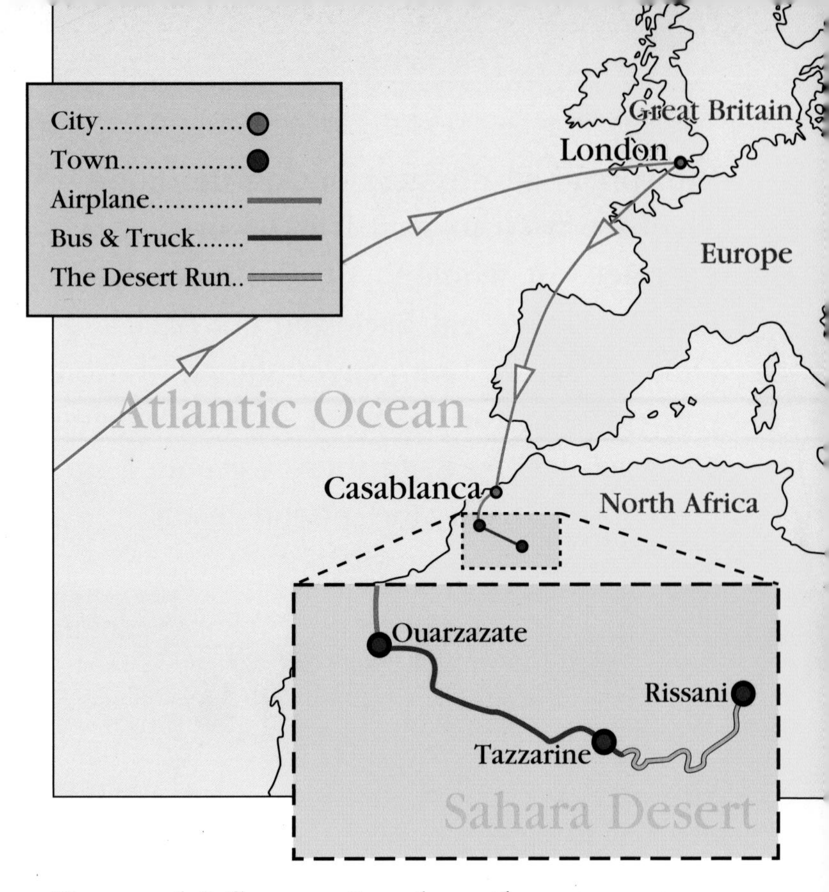

Dan and I flew to London, then to Casablanca, and then over the Atlas Mountains to a place called Ouarzazate*. Then we traveled by bus and truck into the Sahara Desert. It was hot and busy as we settled into the base camp. There were 495 runners from twenty-seven different countries.

* Sounds like **Wah-zah-zart**

The organizers checked everything in our packs. They made sure our medical certificates were OK and gave us a map of the race.

TV helicopters were buzzing around. The flags of all the countries were flying over the starting gate. Dan and I felt proud to see New Zealand's flag. We were the only runners from New Zealand. It was flying because of us.

ATHON
421
MAROC
422
MAROC
207

2. *The Race Starts*

On day one, we had to run 15 miles. The runs would get longer each day.

"Five … four …" everyone joined in the countdown … "three … two … one …" ***Bang!*** went the starting gun.

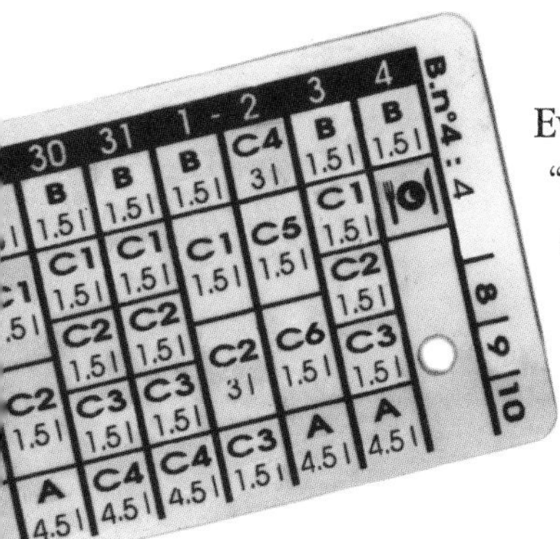

Every runner had to wear a "dog tag." This was clipped at each checkpoint to show we had been given our water.

At the start, my pack didn't feel heavy. I didn't feel the heat or the stony ground. It was just 495 runners charging out, cheering and shouting. But soon the pack was hurting my shoulders. I knew that this was going to be hard work.

Checkpoint 1: 6 miles. We only stopped to refill our water bottles, and then we were off again. I could feel the sun blazing down on my shirt, hat, and arms. I was glad I'd put on plenty of sunblock. The desert began to shimmer in the afternoon heat.

Checkpoint 2: 12 miles. Still going OK.

The “tent crew” had gone on ahead to set up the camp. It was great to see the finishing gate and the balloons as I came over the last hill. And it was great to meet up with the others from my tent and talk about the race. Great to cook up a meal. And great to have a big drink of water.

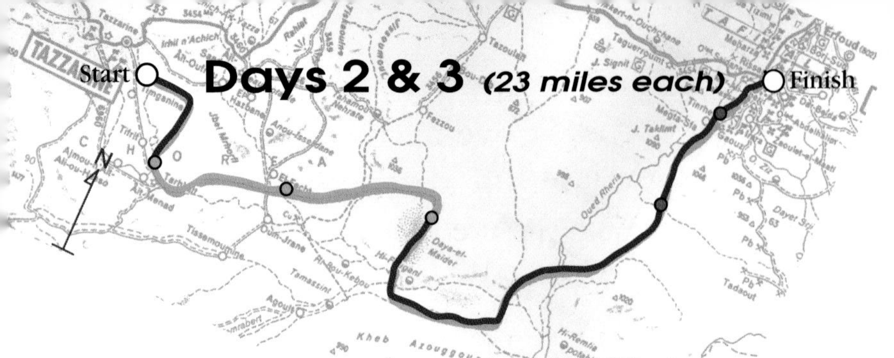

The running was hot and hard. I don't remember much at all. I know I walked in the soft sand and the dunes – I didn't have the energy to run. I didn't feel like I was racing now, except against myself. I just kept going as best I could.

In camp at night, we sat under the stars and talked about the day's run - and bandaged our blistered feet. I was coming about 350th and Dan was about 100th. Now there were 480 left in the race. One of the runners from our tent had collapsed. He and fourteen other runners were out of the race. I felt sad for them, and wondered whether I'd make it.

The camp was quiet that night - not much laughing and joking. We were thinking of the next day's run. The big one.

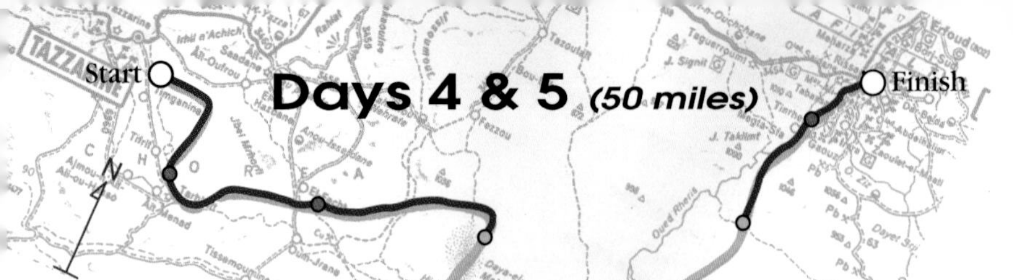

3. *The Big One*

Dan and I wished each other luck. We had two days for this part of the race, which included a night run. Some would take ten hours, others thirty!

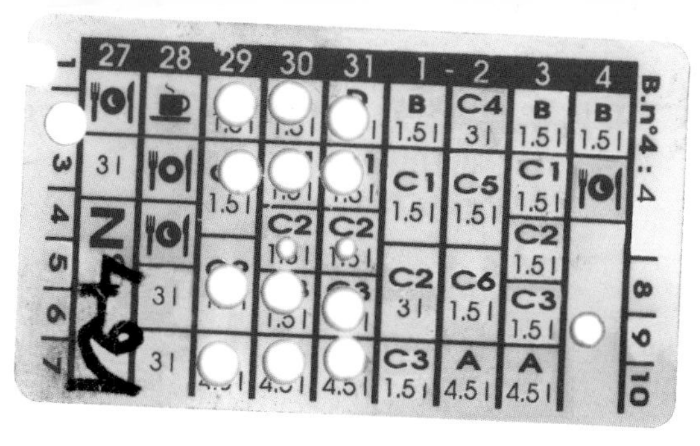

I set off at nine in the morning, jogging through the sand. By halfway through the second leg, it was extremely hot. As I passed one runner, he just seemed to faint. I grabbed him as he fell to the ground. Luckily, a four-wheel drive with some medics in it was coming along.

We got two and a half pints of water at each checkpoint. That sounds a lot, but in the desert you need every drop. If I had any left when I got to a checkpoint, I poured it into my hat to cool my head. That was a luxury!

The sun was setting when I reached checkpoint four. I filled up my water bottles. Then the marshal clipped my dog-tag and checked me off. Some runners were settling down for a meal and a sleep. I almost joined them, but I didn't want to let anyone pass me. I kept going.

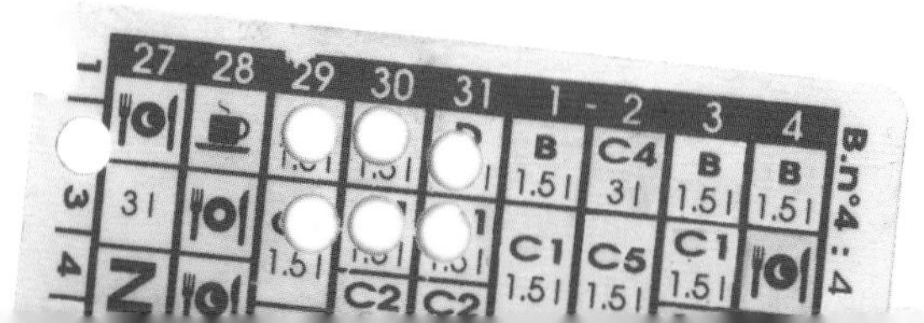

It was hard setting out into the night, away from the lights. I needed my flashlight, and I had to use my compass and the map. There were light-stick markers every mile or so to mark the track.

We were all carrying light sticks for the night run. Sometimes I would see another light bobbing along ahead of me. At other times I felt like I was the only person in the whole desert.

Near the end of the sixth leg, I got lost. I couldn't see any of the markers, just rocky hills and a few dried-up thorn bushes. I used my flashlight to check the map and compass and then kept going. As I came over a hill, I saw the lights of checkpoint six. It was a sight for sore eyes!

Leaving checkpoint five had been hard. Leaving checkpoint six was worse. It was midnight. I had been going for fifteen hours, and I was exhausted. There were sleeping bodies scattered all around. No one seemed to be moving on. I leaned up against some cartons of water bottles and almost fell asleep. But I pulled my pack on again and trudged off into the night. By now I wasn't running. I was doing the "Sahara shuffle."

At a quarter to five in the morning,
I came through a gap in the hills. There
in the distance, twinkling like a far-off city,
was the camp. The balloons were lit up
with spotlights. Two long lines of light
sticks marked the way to the finish gate.
I felt like an airplane coming in to land.
I was weeping as I crossed the line.

I thought, "This is stupid! Why cry now?" But I couldn't help it.

All the runners who had come in before me had hung their light sticks outside their tents. The place was like a fairyland. I crawled into my sleeping bag and collapsed beside Dan.

We smelled terrible, but no one cared. My running shirt was stiff with salt from the sweat. When I scratched my hair, my fingernails went black.

In the evening, the whole camp gathered to cheer in the last stragglers. But another forty-five runners had dropped out. There were 435 left. Dan was coming 70th; I was 331st.

4. *The Finish*

The final two days seemed easy after the 50-mile run. And our packs were getting lighter as we ate our way through the food.

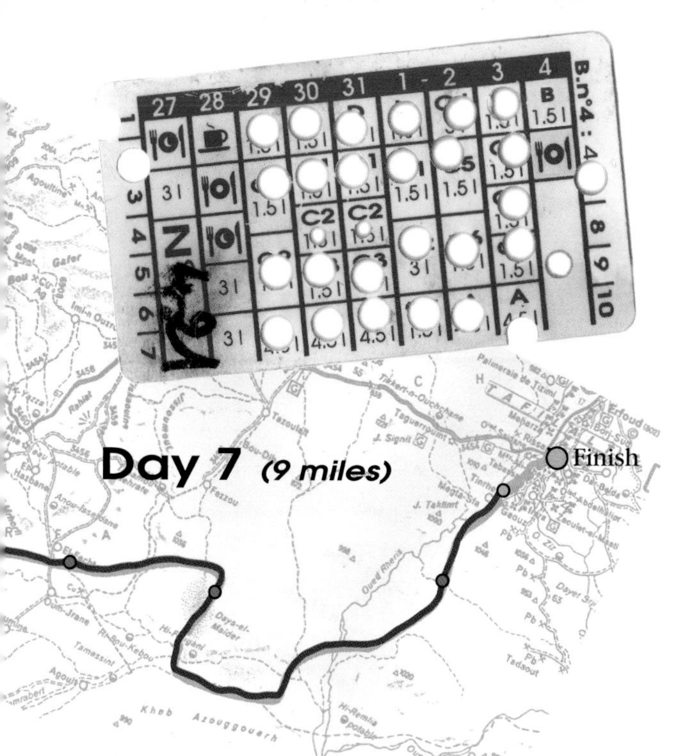

Day 7 - only nine miles! Dan took off like a rocket. I jogged. We were passing through villages. Children ran alongside, asking for sweets and money and especially for pens.

Then there was the finish line, in a town square. There were flags flying, bands playing, and people cheering and laughing.

I grabbed the hand of the nearest runner, a woman from Japan. We crossed the finish line together. Dan had come in 61st. I was 319th, but I didn't care. I was happy to still be standing - happy just to have done it.

13e
MARATHON DES SABLES
27 Mars
6 Avril